TIME MANAGEMENT TECHNIQUES

HOW TO MAKE YOUR TIME COUNT

ANTHONY EKANEM

ISBN 978-1-68487-157-5

Dedicated to my wonderful readers!

Contents

Preface

Do you find yourself rushing through your morning, stampeding to the door, making your way through traffic only to arrive 10 minutes late for work because you had to wait for the train? How does the rest of your day go?

Once you get yourself into work, do you need to take a few moments to compose yourself? Perhaps you get a coffee and relax by chatting with a co-worker on your way to your desk. When you sit down you see five items that need immediate attention (some leftover from yesterday) and the phone starts ringing. You forgot the morning meeting! So, you start rifling through your papers. Is this sounding all too familiar by now?

Regardless of whether you work at home, in an office or a factory, or whether you work for a boss or yourself, getting a grip on time seems like a daily struggle for millions of people.

Are You Overbooked?

Many of us have indeed heaped our daily schedule full of activities. Despite cell phones, the internet, and microwaves, it seems we never have enough time to take care of business, ourselves, our friends, and family.

So many of the activities we do every day are demanding our attention that it can be difficult to make plans, even if the plans will ease our burdens down the road. We are busy but are we productive with our time? This is where time management has become important.

What Will Time Management Do for You?

Time management isn't a physics course, but it is worth making the effort to review and apply in your busy life. Why? Because time management isn't just about having time – it's about making certain our time is well spent. There will always be times in your life when you get extra busy (back to school, taxes, holidays, important projects) but learning the skills to manage the time you have wisely will alleviate much of the stress and frustration that can lead to burnout and fatigue.

Working Smarter – Not Harder

Your time is a valuable resource – both to your employer, business, and family. When you treat every task you do as a priority, it is easy to slip into bad habits that eat into your time which do not give you enough benefits. You run around 'putting out fires' and face every day's activities as emergencies. Nothing is planned and you never have time to get things done properly. Identifying these areas and restructuring your routine and mindset enables you to optimise your time so you produce the most results with the least effort.

How does this work? By identifying daily routines and your "body rhythms", you can try to plan the most energy-consuming activities during your most productive times of the day and use your less productive times for activities that do not require the same amount of concentration or effort.

This applies equally well to all parts of your life – work and home. But it goes beyond that. Time management also helps you identify time (or energy) wasters. Perhaps some activities must be removed or delegated to someone else. By learning how to identify these, you will not succumb to guilty feelings that you were not "up to the job" but you will conscientiously decide that to keep doing them is a waste of valuable resource – your time.

Time Management is a Skill

You are not at boot camp. Although the discipline encouraged by boot camps may be useful, it does not relate well to daily life. Work and family usually call for flexibility and learning the skill of time management will allow you to make wise choices without being tied to a strict routine.

Would your boss be pleased if you turned down an important assignment presented to you with urgency by hearing you say, "I have a strict schedule to follow, and tomorrow is my filing day so I cannot accept another assignment at this time"? Or would your daughter, having forgotten to mention her soccer game until the night before, be satisfied with "we planned to do the laundry, remember? It's on the schedule."

Developing time management skills with the help of this book will show you how to determine what tasks need to be done and when they are in harmony with your overall goals at work and home.

You Can Make Last-Minute Decisions

That means when you have a last-minute invitation out for a 'couples only' supper on Friday night, but you've already booked up the weekend for family activities, you will determine whether one more social activity will contribute to your happiness as a couple or drain you for the family activities you planned for the weekend.

When your supervisor asks you to help with some backed up invoicing, you can determine if giving a helpful hand to an important part of the business will improve your reputation as a team player or will cause other, equally important jobs that have already been assigned to you, to become delayed or jeopardized.

Making conscious decisions about why you use the time the way you do will prevent you from appearing incapable or feeling overwhelmed. You will have the confidence to give your answers (even if it's a 'no') without questioning your judgment.

If you say no to a task, you will be able to furnish an explanation as to why you are making that decision if need be. Or in the case of an employer or manager, you can explain your situation and allow them to decide which task uses your time to the most profitable ends. You may find that they were unaware of your current load and are thankful that you are concerned about making the best use of your time and talents.

You Will Have a Purpose in What You Do

While time management is a skill that should be used day-to-day, it is also useful to help reach your long-term goals. Your goals may be hazy right now, or even obscure, but by incorporating them into the 'why' of what you do every day, you will be making strides to accomplish them while enjoying what you do.

Even the drudgery that sometimes comes with life is easier to manage if you know why you must do it. Knowing why will make these chores a part of your plan, and thus a choice rather than a burden. Managing your time can also prevent these areas from becoming dragged out and thus affecting your usefulness and energy.

Getting Started

The first step to getting your time managed is to find out exactly how much your time is worth.

CHAPTER ONE

How Much is Your Time Worth?

What does an hour of your time cost? While every dollar has the same value, every hour does not. An hour at 10:00 in the morning may be of much more value as a working hour than 11:00 at night. On the other hand, an hour at your child's bedside when he is sick is worth more than an hour at the office catching up on your filing.

However, most of us recognize that an hour at work is an hour at work and if you will be there for eight or 12 hours, you want those hours to be used productively so they don't become extra hours catching up to missed deadlines or preventing you from spending time with your family.

There are two methods for determining the value of your time.

- What Does an Hour Cost Your Employer?
- What Does an Hour Cost YOU?

What Does an Hour Cost Your Employer?

If you work for someone, you must realize that the activities you do cost the business more than just your hourly wage. You need to account for the cost of overhead and the percentage of income that you are responsible to provide for.

If you are a salaried employee, you can take your salary (month or year) and add the cost of the office space, equipment, or other costs as you presume them to be. Divide this number by the number of hours you would work in an average month or year. A month gives you approximately 20 working days. A year has about 240.

The resulting figure is what an hour costs. Now, when you are deciding to do an activity, you can determine if the task at hand is worth that number of resources to the business – your time and physical resources. You might be surprised.

Raise Your Value

Don't think your time is worth that much? Don't base it purely on what others have valued it at – raise your value and you will reap the rewards. Work like you are paid more and you will surely stand out from the crowd. You will be more productive and waste less time.

What if you cost your business $5 per minute instead of $5 per hour. Or $10 per minute instead of $10 per hour. How much would time be worth now? Would you hang around an office waiting room or stay on hold on the telephone? Or would you confirm appointments and leave messages. Raising your value will improve how you view your time and will help you spend your time productively.

What Does an Hour Cost YOU?

Are you self-employed or on contract? This makes it more imperative that you spend your time wisely in that it can have an immediate impact on your income.

How much is your time worth (billing hour)? Now create a list of activities that are not directly related to creating income such as book-keeping, website maintenance, cleaning, etc. Based on the previous month, how many hours were spent doing each task?

If you bill $30 per hour for your service and you spend 15 hours per month maintaining your website, it has cost you $450 that month. It may also have cost you 15 more hours away from your family and friends or impeded actual production time. If having an up-to-date website is crucial to your business (but is not the actual business) then perhaps you would do better to pay someone to maintain it for you. It will give you more time for important tasks and may be accomplished in less time if the person is more skilled than yourself.

The Value of Your Time - Beyond Money

Time management goes beyond knowing the monetary value of your time – your time also has value.

Unlike money, each hour of your day does not have the same value. You cannot always use money or profits as a factor when determining how much your time is worth. Your life is made up of people, interests, and caring for yourself and others. Basing your time merely on the amount of money you will make or save is missing the big picture.

Have you ever heard someone answer the question "if you had six months to live, what would you do" with the answer "make more money"? Unless they had nagging financial concerns about their family, most people would acknowledge that time spent bettering oneself, spent with family, and showing interest in others has greater value.

When your child has a school event he wants you to attend or you haven't spent one evening all week to rest up and relax, you need to determine the value of your time in the context of living a productive life – not just making money.

Working For Yourself – Drawing the Line

If you are self-employed or tend to take a lot of work home with you, it is important to ask yourself if the time you spend on certain tasks is worth the sacrifice of time doing other things.

While it can be difficult to make decisions about how you use your time when you feel the pressure to perform many tasks, it's not impossible. Take the time to assess your goals and make decisions that reflect them.

While being reliable is important you may find new strategies that make better use of your time. You can identify areas where you should be delegating instead of doing things yourself. You might try reorganizing your day, so your schedule includes the most important tasks you need to accomplish while fitting less important tasks around it.

Taking the time to understand the value of your time now is going to save you frustration in the future. The following chapters will help you identify goals, set a schedule, and identify habits that may be costing you more than just time.

CHAPTER TWO

Where Does the Time Go?

You've tried this before – creating a "To-Do" list, scheduling some appointments, and booking projects. You have started the day on the right footing, determined to get on top of things.

The children's lunches were packed and ready. You had plenty of time to get to work in the morning without any stress. When you arrived at work, your projects were in order, your day timer up-to-date and you knew exactly where you need to be and when.

Because you used a schedule, you figured that you'd have no problem getting everything done on time. You start alright, but as you carry on through the day, you notice the time and are shocked that you only accomplished half of what you planned before you must switch activities. Several interruptions by co-workers and clients and before you realize it the schedule has been abandoned and you are again rushing through your activities and feeling overwhelmed. Why does this happen?

You Have More Time Than You Think

Before you blame the scheduling process, you need to see what other factors affect your day. You can do this by logging your normal routine for a few days. It is difficult to appreciate the time you spend on activities that do not contribute to your productivity until you've logged them over a few days.

Creating a Log

For the next few days, keep a pen and paper handy to write down what you're doing and the time when you change activities. Quickly assess and write down how you feel – energetic, tired, hungry, or anything else you can identify. This record does not have to be detailed but should include every activity change in your workday.

Identifying Patterns

After you've kept a log for a couple of days, you will be able to analyze certain patterns. Do you often feel tired in the middle of the afternoon? Are you refreshed after taking a small lunch? Did you spend longer on menial tasks or talking to others than you thought? How many people used up your time with little benefit (phone calls, drop-ins, and emails)?

Finding these patterns can help you plan your activities so they fit better with your natural rhythms. Perhaps you find getting through the afternoon (or getting started in the morning) to be the most draining. Is it possible to schedule your most challenging projects or meetings when you are most alert and energetic? Block off this time in your schedule – no calls, no meetings – so that you can accomplish the most work.

Give Yourself Rewards

You can also try implementing a self-reward program when needed. If pushing through a tedious project causes you to dawdle or get easily distracted, you might find that giving yourself small rewards as you complete small chunks of work will keep you motivated.

Perhaps you will only get a cup of coffee when you've finished filing half of the pile. Or maybe you'll take a stretch or call a friend (briefly) when you've dealt with 20 emails. Keep the rewards small but frequent enough to keep your momentum and prevent you from resorting to distractions which will only prolong the process.

Should You Stop Wasting Time?

This process may also highlight to you that after evaluating how much your time is worth you should consider delegating some of your work to other people or eliminating some tasks.

While it is commendable to keep on top of things, you may be wasting resources by trying to do everything yourself. Smaller businesses frequently call on the owner or employees to wear several hats during the day or week. While it appears to cut costs, this may be wasting resources. Perhaps hiring someone part-time to help with the filing, cleaning and mailouts would permit key employees to spend their time in more profitable occupations.

If you identify this problem and you are an employee, you need to discuss your findings with your manager or employer. If approached properly they may see that your time is better spent focused on aspects of your job that are more profitable. Important duties are being compromised by menial tasks that need to be performed.

Whatever you discover to be a time waster, you must take steps to deal with. Here are some ideas for four common time wasters.

Top Time Wasters

MEETINGS:people in meetings all day are not getting things done.

Meetings have their place. They are an important way to deal with group issues, create plans, and get feedback. What is a problem is when meetings are called on the spur of the moment with little preparation and no plan. When these meetings start each person has a separate agenda. If the purpose is unclear and the participants unprepared, are you going to come to a clear decision?

To avoid wasting time with meetings try the following:

1) Create an agenda giving each item a time allotment – Prioritize the agenda so the most important issues are dealt with first.

2) Send the agenda to each participant so they can come prepared.

3) Focus on getting a solution – scheduling another meeting should not be the solution although it may be a part of completing the plan.

4) Avoid last-minute meetings

5) Schedule meetings for the end of the day or week so that all involved can arrange their workflow and jump right into their tasks the next morning.

6) If the issue can be dealt with on the phone or through email don't plan a meeting.

PHONE CALLS: You don't have to answer every time it rings.

If you have blocked a certain time for working on a task do not let phone calls interrupt your momentum. While you may feel that you need always be 'on-call' the truth is that you are losing productivity by permitting continual interruptions to your workflow.

If you must answer the call and the person can wait, ask them for a time when you can call back and discuss the issue. Not only will you set boundaries with your time, but you can be prepared to deal with the call without other distractions.

To avoid wasting time with phone calls try the following:

1) Turn off your phone for two hours while you complete your task. If that is too much, then do it for one hour or 30 minutes.

2) Ask that your calls be held for the allotted time (making exceptions for those who need it – like your boss).

3) If you answer tell the person you are in the middle of a task, so you need to schedule a return call later that day. Decide who will make the return call and when.

DROP-IN VISITORS: "Do You Have a Minute" will always take longer.

If you cannot finish a task without a co-worker stopping in to ask you for a minute of your time you may find your whole day is occupied with 'one-minute' issues. Often the individual will get comfortable and discuss many more items than the one they initially came to you with.

While some positions do require an open-door policy, or you may not have an office you can close the door to, it is important to have uninterrupted time in your day to complete the tasks on your list.

To avoid wasting time with 'drop-ins' try the following:

1) Schedule the time you are not available, so YOU stand by your decision

2) Close the door or use a 'do-not-disturb' sign to discourage idle visitors.

3) If you must deal with a situation or individual, ask for the details and suggest you find a time to sit down and discuss it. Schedule it so they know you view it as important and want to give them your time.

Working at the WRONG TIME: Wasting Your Resources

Are you always planning activities that clash with other people's schedules? Do you find the time you allotted to make calls (such as lunchtime) means you are not able to get a hold of anyone? Do you ask for help when everyone else is too busy?

Rearranging your schedule to make the most of your time will prevent you from 'getting in your way'. Find the most opportune times for tasks and your day will be much more productive.

To avoid wasting time with bad scheduling try the following:

1) Do you find more people available to talk to later in the day? Make all your return calls then.

2) Do you often need to ask for assistance with big projects? Plan so that your project does not conflict with other people's schedules.

3) Give yourself extra lead time. Things don't always work out as you plan, give yourself some extra time so you can make your deadlines even if you have setbacks. Check up on delegated tasks to make sure they're on schedule and give them early deadlines as well.

Disorganized WORKSPACE:

To use your time well it is a MUST that you have an organized workspace. Every moment looking for a pen, a file, or a misplaced check not only means wasted time, but it can add to your stress level and interfere with your ability to focus on your work.

To avoid wasting time with a disorganized workspace:

1) Give EVERYTHING a home. This includes your cell phone and keys.

2) Keep daily needs easily accessible. Whether you work from your car or an office, place phone lists, calendars, and other daily-needed items in an easy-to-see

spot, or an easily accessible folder.

3) Put everything else away. Files and tools that are not in use need to be put away. The easiest way to do that is to give yourself at least 50% more storage space than you currently need. If you cram items into a small space, you will not likely keep up with your organizing and you will have difficulty finding what you need.

Once you've identified and dealt with key time wasters you will be surprised how much more productive your day can be!

CHAPTER THREE

Setting Goals

One of the key ingredients for successfully managing your time is identifying your goals. Goals are what will keep you motivated and focused – both essential to being productive.

What do goals have to do with time management?

When you have determined where you want your life to be in one year – or five – or even 20, it will have an impact on what you do TODAY. A person who dreams of being a lawyer will not have much success obtaining that goal if they don't first take the time to fit studying and school into their schedule today.

Many long-term goals will have short-term goals that lead to them. Not only does this make practical sense (that is, getting accepted to university is a shorter-term goal than becoming a partner in a law firm) but it also helps you from becoming overwhelmed or losing sight of your goals.

If you are trying to manage your time it is because you recognize that there is a limited supply, and it is all valuable. While responsibilities at work and home may be what dictates how you plan your day, shouldn't all (or most) of this time work in harmony with your goals? This may mean some big changes, or it may just mean adjusting some things in your routine.

When you start planning your time with a goal in mind it is easier to appreciate the benefits of what you are doing and prevents you from getting caught up in time wasters – activities that use up your time but are ultimately unprofitable either in money or your personal life.

Choosing Goals Wisely

If you are currently making $5 per hour and can't cover your bills you may decide that your goal needs to be making more money. Take some time to figure out exactly what you'd like to be doing with your life. Acknowledge that this may mean spending time getting an education rather than taking on another low-paying job that will fill your financial needs but keep you in a cycle of working endless hours to make the money you need.

Or maybe you find your work time is eating into the time you want to spend with your family. That family will grow and move away so what you do to make more time for them is important NOW. Identifying these goals will help you make decisions to make better use of your time.

Setting Long Term Goals

Before you say "my goal is to retire to the Caribbean" it is important to take stock and analyze your situation from a different perspective. While you may truly be able to retire to the Caribbean, HOW will you do that? A new job? A higher income? Fewer responsibilities?

Long-term goals are excellent motivators. They help you see beyond today's work and remind you that there is a greater purpose for the time you are spending today. If you find a task tedious you should think about how doing it fits into your goals. Making your daily tasks become choices can ease some of the burdens because we are in control of our day rather than having it control us.

On the other hand, if we realize many of the time-consuming activities, we do have no bearing on reaching our goals perhaps we have to take them out or at least reduce the time we spend on them.

Your long-term goal may be to spend more time with your family. Make your goal specific and give it a date to be accomplished. Perhaps you are determined to work part-time. Write down the date this will take effect and put it on your calendar. It may be that you anticipate it will take two years to achieve this goal. Pick a date and put it where you can see it every day. Now you must set short-term goals.

Setting Short Term Goals

Your short-term goals will relate to your long-term goal. Continuing with our illustration of working part-time, you may decide that you must first complete certain projects you have already committed to. You will also need to be more selective about what assignments you can handle or need to ask for an assistant so you can focus on the main business and get help with minor tasks.

You may set a date to stop working overtime. You may set a date to ask for contract work instead of salary. You should plan activities that are spent with family and have no work interruptions. Whatever your goals they should be clear steps to achieving your long-term goal: spending more time with family.

These short-term goals will help you measure your progress towards your long-term goal. They will shape how you plan your time and clarify the VALUE of your time. Make your goals specific and give them a date to be completed.

Steps to Creating Achievable Goals:

With every goal you must follow the 6 Ps:

1. **Prioritize:**You may have several goals. Prioritize them on your list.

2. **Positive:**Use positive language. "I will ...", "I'll be...", "I'll have..."

3. **Precise:**Be precise. "I will have supper with my family three nights a week" rather than "I will be home earlier"

4. **Performance:**Measure your performance. Set time for starting and completing your goal. "May 1 – I will be home at 5:30 three nights this week"

5. **Practical:**Make your goals practical. Do you have the control to make this work, or do you rely on other people to meet your goal?

6. **Personal:**Is this goal a personal goal or someone else's desire for you?

Time management is easier when you can motivate yourself and judge the value of your time. If your goals are based on someone else's desires (if your mate wants you to work in a steady job but you want to be self-employed) you will find it difficult to manage your time due to a lack of motivation.

Creating an Action Plan

Your action plan will have a great deal to do with your day-to-day schedule. Now that you have made yourself conscious of where you are headed (long term goal) and have set up guideposts (short term goals) it will merely mean implementing an action plan to get your time on track.

Use your short-term goals to implement your action plan. If you are not making radical changes but are just trying to take the stress out of your day you will find the time you took to think about your goals may be enough to keep your priorities in order.

If you find that you need to refocus on your goals, you will need to give each short-term goal a date to start or complete – write it down.

Within the time frame of the goal write down the actions that need to be taken to realize the goal. If you have discovered from the exercises above that you need to hire an assistant this may mean putting out an ad, reviewing resumes, conducting interviews, hiring, and training. Each task must be assigned a time to complete.

The action plan combined with a focus on goals will help you appreciate the overall effects of valuing your time. In this example, you will realize that even though you may need to use MORE time this month by interviewing and training an assistant – your GOAL to spend less time on minor tasks is being accomplished. At this point, your time is valued compared to your goal. In a month you will be spending less time with minor matters even if it requires more work at the early stage.

Resources

Part of your Action Plan should include a summary of the resources you need to meet your goals. An assistant is a resource, more education is a resource, a supportive mate is a resource. List the resources you need to obtain and include them in your action plan – when will you get them and how will they be obtained?

Review and Update

While writing goals down is an effective tool for managing your time you will still need to review and update them occasionally.

Perhaps you encounter an unexpected obstacle on your way to meeting your long-term goal. Reassess and determine if you can adapt your action plan. If you cannot adapt your plan you will need to consider why the plan went off course – did you have less power to control the situation than you thought? Were you unaware of some of the resources you would need and their cost or time obligations?

Use this new information to reconsider your goal. Is it still attainable or do you need to adjust it – either by lengthening the time or changing the outcome – and devising a new action plan?

CHAPTER FOUR

Making the Most of Your Time

Before you determine that you can't live by a schedule, consider what happens when you don't.

The 80/20 Rule

The 80/20 rule is a common ratio used to determine performance versus resources. It is a general assumption that we use 80% of our resources (time, money, skill) to achieve 20% of our performance. The opposite is also true – we use 20% of our resources to achieve 80% of our performance.

It is impossible to suggest that any person can be 100% productive 100% of the time. We all have our most productive times of the day, activities, and abilities. By using the processes outlined earlier you should be able to pinpoint the most productive times of the day, the most valuable use for your time, and your priorities.

Now you need to recognize that to use your time to the fullest you want to find ways of increasing that 20% to 30%, 40%, or even more. When you identify the most productive times of the day and schedule your top producing activities into those times and make that task a priority you've already reset your thinking and will be working smarter –

not harder.

The 'To-Do' List

The 'To-Do' list is not just for list-making junkies. If you find that tasks are not being accomplished on time or even forgotten you need a 'to-do' list.

How detailed you make the list is up to you but every task that is given to you should have the following recorded with it:

When does it need to be completed?

How long will it take to do?

How important is it?

When will I do it?

At the end of the day make a list of tasks that need to be accomplished the following day. Prioritize them according to importance. Give each task an earlier deadline and 50% more time to complete than you think.

As soon as you start your workday you will know exactly what needs doing and when. If you have booked some uninterrupted time, you will have no problem accomplishing your highest priority tasks. Tasks that do not get completed will be reassigned for another day, delegated to someone else, or removed from your list.

Get in the habit of creating a 'To-Do' list each day. It may be easier to keep this on your computer or PDA so that you can easily re-schedule activities without writing them over onto a new sheet.

Prioritizing

Not every task can be completed in a day. Your schedule will just become another 'task' in your day unless you learn to prioritize. Prioritizing ensures that what NEEDS to be done is done.

When you are handed a new assignment, you should immediately put it on your 'To-Do' list. Number the tasks on your list so that number '1' is most important and work down from there.

Take your top three priorities and schedule them into your weekly or monthly planner. Write down your deadline (always a few days early!) and block off time to get it done. If it requires collaboration with others, schedule that too. You may have to make some appointments when you know where you are at with the task, but it is important to write something down so that you don't overbook.

After the top three priorities have been given their spots in your schedule start adding the others. Schedule the most important tasks first. Keep your schedule with enough time to manage day-to-day activities like reading emails and returning phone calls. Plan on 50% more time to finish each task than you think necessary.

Each day will now have a list of scheduled activities that consider the priority of individual tasks. Use this to create your daily 'To-Do' list.

Scheduling Low Priority Tasks

As you see your schedule filling up with high-priority tasks you will need to make some decisions about your low-priority tasks. If you have scheduled low-priority tasks into your day but have had to move them onto the following day's to-do list, they will quickly become bigger and more of a priority as you continue to put them off.

One way to prevent this is to use the 'one more task' philosophy. Every day try to do one more task than you planned or scheduled. One more phone call or 10 minutes of filing will keep these tasks from becoming daunting.

If that is not working you may determine that these activities need to be delegated. Valuing your time requires decisiveness. These tasks keep your work moving along and if they are ignored it can cause a huge interference. Think of looking for a file when a client calls, and you see that it is in a pile of 50 others. You will be losing the effects of time management by not dealing with these issues right away.

Action Plans

Action plans are not to be confused with 'To-Do' lists or schedules. Action plans are the itemized tasks you need to follow to complete a goal. You completed this activity in an earlier chapter.

Sit down and determine what actions are needed to accomplish your goal. Who do you need to meet with? What resources do you need? Where do you have to go?

The Action Plan will be a crucial tool for your scheduling purposes. If you have not planned your actions your schedule may be flawed if you did not make time or plans to accomplish the goal.

CHAPTER FIVE

Special Tips for Family Time Management

The goal-oriented process of time management works equally well in family time management as it does for work-related time management. How can you adapt these processes to the unique needs of family time management?

Get Everyone on the Same Page

You won't be able to manage the family's time if you have one or two members who won't cooperate. Sit down with everyone and explain that everybody is busy, but we will all be happier and get more of what we want if everybody can work together.

Make sure that everybody sees the benefit – meals won't be so late, and appointments won't be missed if everyone does their best to keep to a schedule. That means that school appointments and extracurricular activities MUST be put on the schedule as soon as they know about them.

Respecting each other's time will mean that everyone gets a fair chance. If schedules overlap it is time to reorganize or eliminate activities.

Make it Fun

Planning is easier when it's fun. Get a large wall calendar or a laminated blank calendar and put the dates in. Get everyone together and assign a coloured marker to everyone. Have everyone write their activities and times on the calendar (or have them tell you while you fill it in).

Every time a new appointment is made the family is required to mark it down or tell you so you can fill it in. This will prevent double-booking the car or a parent's time and the coloured markers will identify if one person is demanding more of the family's time and resources than the others.

If you are a parent and you see that your children's schedules are packed with extracurricular activities, it might be wise to limit them to once or twice a week. This is especially true if homework and projects are interfering with sleep, meals, and other family time.

Teaching your kids to keep a balanced schedule not only promotes good time management habits they will need in college and work life, but it impresses on them that taking care of responsibilities and spending unstructured time together is part of a balanced life.

If everyone is dashing off in different directions all the time put mealtime into the schedule as well as a family night. Both children and adults can then plan their activities so that most nights the family can be together for at least a part of the evening.

List – so you don't forget!

If you have the room, make a note on the calendar of the items needed for each activity or appointment. If there's no room, you can list the activities elsewhere along with the needed items. Keep it next to the calendar and you can quickly see what needs to go with whom.

Remind each person the night before to have the necessary items ready – sports equipment, musical instruments, documents, etc. Lists like this can also be used to make weekly meals run on time and with less stress.

Have each person tell you a meal that they enjoy. Put it on a Master list of meal ideas. Leave the list on the fridge or somewhere that the family can add to it when they think of something.

Later, take the list and create a shopping list for the meals. Each week you can choose the meals you will make for the week and will already have a list of all the ingredients you need to make them. Take the list with you when you go grocery shopping, and not only will you know what you're making each night but you'll be sure to have all the necessary ingredients to make it.

Spending a little time preparing will help you stay organized and prevent you or other family members from forgetting items and appointments – a real time waster.

Household Chores

Just like work the home has many tasks vying for your attention: dishes, laundry, meal preparation, vacuuming, etc. Use the same prioritizing process as outlined. Make a 'to-do list. Prioritize the list (laundry needs doing every week, daily bed-making can sometimes go undone). Schedule the tasks on your calendar so small tasks don't become overwhelming ones.

On your 'to-do' list put the top priorities for the week. Daily jobs should also be listed according to priority. While you may let one or two daily tasks slip if it becomes a regular habit you'll need to determine: delegate or remove?

If you delegate, you should decide if a family member will do it or you'll hire the job out. If it's removed perhaps the job can be done less frequently (maybe the carpets don't need vacuuming EVERY day). An undone task will drain you mentally. Decide if and how it's to be done and move on.

If your children are old enough to help, use the coloured marker system and book them for meal making, dishwashing, garbage collecting, etc. Plan a reward at the end of the week for those who accomplished all the tasks. While your children must learn that helping the family is not a favour, they respond as we do to rewarding tedious work with small bonuses.

Using the Goal system, choose a family goal – perhaps it's a new DVD player or a trip to the zoo. Put the reward on the schedule with a big sticker or another eye-catching marking. Your children are sure to see it every time they look at the calendar. If they complete all their tasks without nagging for four weeks in a row – the trip to the zoo. Three months – new DVD player.

Don't forget smaller goals. Each week can mean that if the children do all their chores, they pick the movie if they don't, then you do. Everyone still benefits but they get more of what they want when they stick to the schedule.

Organizing Makes it Easier

If the clothes don't fit in the dresser, do you expect them to stay off the floor? The same is true for toys, shoes, dishes, videos, and other items. If you are spending time moving piles from one place to another, stacking items, or manipulating them to fit into their storage area, you are wasting time.

Can't keep the kids' coats off the floor? How have you arranged for them to put them away? Hangers in tall closets may not be enough, providing hooks at their level can make it easy and fun for your children to hang up backpacks, coats, and other items like the dog leash.

Art materials, mail, toys, and shoes do better in bins. Lining up items or arranging them in piles is time-consuming and usually doesn't get done regularly. Stop frustrating yourself by providing 'homes' for these items. A bin for each person's shoes lined up under a bench makes it easy for everyone to find what they need (and put it back).

A small basket for mail gives it a 'home' so that school notices and bills don't mysteriously disappear. Art supplies and small toys can be put in labelled bins making them easy to find and a snap to clean up.

Think about areas in your home that cause the most frustration and determine if you are spending too much time maintaining them. Is there a way to make household maintenance less stressful and time consuming for everyone? Spend the money and take the time to organize it – it will be well worth it.

CHAPTER SIX

More Than a Schedule

Goal setting, action plans, to-do lists, and schedules will all combine to help you make the most of your time. But there is something else you need to do... You must commit.

What does commitment mean? It means that you want to take charge of your time. You value the hours in a day, and you want them spent in the most productive way possible. It means that you will get your work done early and produce better quality. You will spend your time as you decide, and your personal life will be spent with a focus on your family and friends instead of your work.

Here are some 'Success' Secrets

Value Time:

Don't waste your time or others. Don't wait around or pursue time-consuming activities that give you little benefit. Don't let phone calls and visits interrupt your workflow.

Prepare and Plan:

Nothing wastes time like lack of direction. Plan your goals and activities and prepare others for your expectations. Expect delays and plan to have extra time to accommodate them.

Know Your Work Habits:

Find out when you work best. What activities affect how productive you are? Watch for and get rid of unproductive habits. Delegate or remove tasks when needed.

Be a Problem Solver:

Complaining wastes time. Find a solution or find help and get it done.

Get the Hard Work Done First:

Don't procrastinate. Start with the difficult work first so you can relax with the easy tasks. Work that remains undone will drain you of energy and slow your progress.

Review Your Progress:

Compare what you have done with what you planned to do. What worked? What made you feel good? What could have been done better?

And lastly, remember that being busy does not equal productivity. You don't just want to get the work finished you want to have it done right. You don't need to complete every task, just arrange that they are dealt with by someone or decide that they do not need doing. You will be judged on how well and timely your work was done, not by how many hours you worked.

Time Management Sheets

Use the following forms to follow the outlined procedures.

ACTION PLAN

State your long-term goal and follow with your short-term goals and the task necessary to complete them. Give definite dates and times to start and complete. List the resources you will need to accomplish them.

Use your action plan to schedule the tasks needed to accomplish your goals. Review it to determine if you are meeting your goals or have allowed other activities and tasks to take over your time.

ACTIVITY LOG

Use one sheet per day and log for one week the daily activities you do and how you feel. List the start times of each activity and write down a new start time each time you change activities.

While you do not have to state your mood for each activity try to establish a pattern by listing at least every hour how you feel: tired, hungry, excited, stressed, etc. The more detailed your log the easier it will be to see patterns emerge.